S0-FQW-922

Blood Pressure Diary

KEEPING IT SIMPLE

Be well!
Renee LaVineen
2017

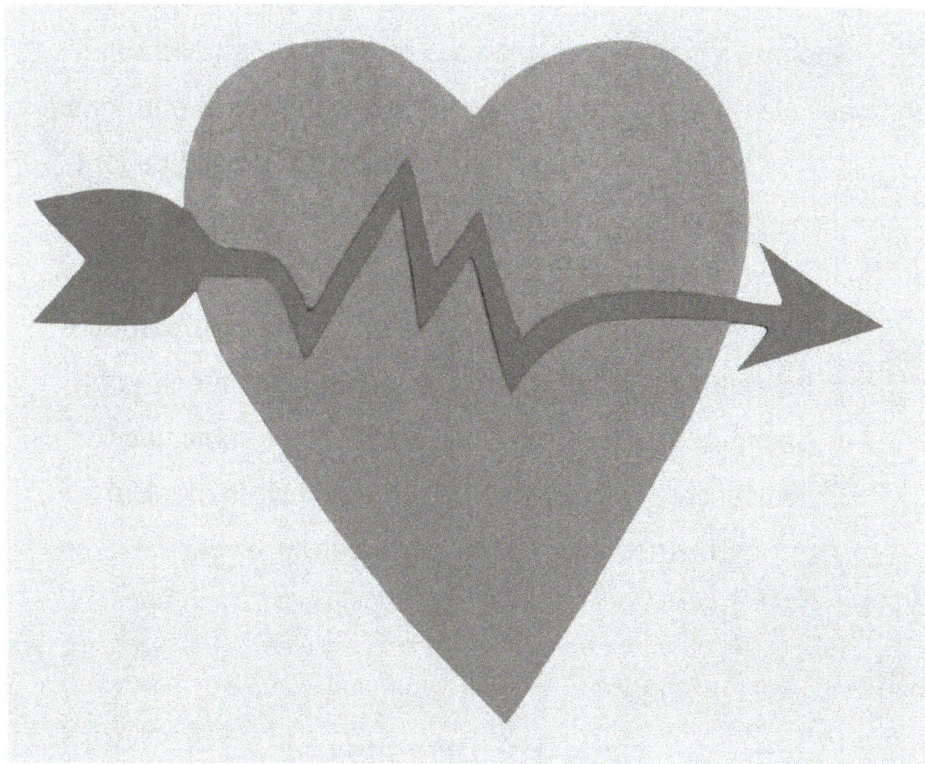

Blood Pressure Diary
KEEPING IT SIMPLE

Copyright © 2017 – Renee' La Viness

All rights reserved. No part of this book may be used
or reproduced in any manner whatsoever without written
permission by the author, except by medical professionals
who may copy pages which are more than half-filled with
medical information about their patient solely for the purpose
of collecting/compiling said information about said patient,
or for brief quotations in critical articles or reviews.

The content of this book was created for the sole purpose
of collecting and storing information. It is not intended to
diagnose or treat any medical conditions or substitute for
medical care. If you believe you may have a medical
problem, contact your health care provider.

ISBN-10: 1977889794

ISBN-13: 978-1977889799

Dedications

To my wonderful family
and all my friends:
You make my life
worth living.

To users of this book:
I hope
this diary
helps you
live your lives
with more joy
and confidence.

Be well.

Acknowledgements

I am so thankful to my long-time doctor J. M. Ritze, my cardiologist J. M. Cassidy, and their very patient staff members. Without them, I am certain I would not be alive. They have helped me through great anxiety and frustration as my heart and I have recovered over the past twelve years. It has been a long journey, and we are not done.

Also, I'd like to acknowledge my favorite pharmacist, Henry. Until I learned I could order my medications early, he suffered through so many of my panic attacks with true class. He has always had a smile and a kind word of support, encouragement, and comfort when I needed them most. His patience and understanding have meant so much.

I don't think any of these people realize how much Gene and I appreciate them. These words seem insignificant when compared to the care and compassion I've received, but they come from the deepest depths of <u>my</u> <u>heart</u>.

INTRODUCTION

THE SHORT & SKINNY ON BLOOD PRESSURE

Your blood pressure changes constantly. Deadlines, stress, foods, insufficient sleep... many things can affect it. How much it is affected might depend on your age, diet, daily exercise, and other factors. High (or low) blood pressure may be signs of serious health problems. Ask your doctor what numbers are right for you.

HOW TO USE THIS BOOK

Write your **name** and **start date** on the spine of this book, so the most recent one is easy to find on the bookshelf.

Record your blood pressure, heart rate (pulse), and other notes on the designated pages. If there is not enough room, continue onto the back of the page, which is blank. When you suspect something might be affecting your blood pressure, or you have a problem, write those things in the notes. You can also make notes about exercise, stress, what you've eaten, when you took your medicine or vitamins, a blood sugar reading, and more.

Keep the medical information pages updated. In an emergency, it could make the difference in the speed and quality of your health care.

> **Tell your family and friends where you keep this book. Ask them to help you remember it when visiting the doctor or hospital, especially in an emergency.**

NAME _Sample Smith_

DATE	TIME	BLOOD PRESSURE	PULSE	NOTES
1-1-17	2:00 AM/**PM**	110 / 76	70	
	7:00 AM/**PM**	114 / 82	73	
1-2	9:00 **AM**/PM	130 / 85	75	stressful morning. Dog →
	2:00 AM/**PM**	108 / 72	68	
	7:00 AM/**PM**	115 / 80	72	
1-3	9:00 **AM**/PM	122 / 83	70	
	2:15 AM/**PM**	106 / 70	72	
	7:00 AM/**PM**	112 / 82	68	
1-4	9:00 **AM**/PM	110 / 74	68	
	11:00 **AM**/PM	135 / 95	75	Felt strange. Light-headed, dizzy.
	11:20 **AM**/PM	108 / 75	68	After I threw up. Better now.
	2:00 AM/**PM**	108 / 73	70	
	7:20 AM/**PM**	110 / 80	71	
1-5	9:00 **AM**/PM	105 / 77	68	
	2:00 AM/**PM**	107 / 73	70	
	7:00 AM/**PM**	113 / 82	70	
	AM/PM	/	-	
	AM/PM	/	-	
	AM/PM	/	-	
	AM/PM	/	-	
	AM/PM	/	-	
	AM/PM	/	-	
	AM/PM	/	-	
	AM/PM	/	-	

chased newspaper guy. I chased dog. No time for breakfast.

SAMPLE

IMPORTANT MEDICAL INFORMATION

NAME _____ AGE _____ DOB _____ BLOOD TYPE _____

ADDRESS _____

PHONE(S) _____

EMERGENCY CONTACTS

NAME / RELATION_____PHONE_____

NAME / RELATION_____PHONE_____

DOCTOR_____PHONE_____

DOCTOR_____PHONE_____

PHARMACY_____ PHONE_____

INS._____POLICY/GROUP#_____PRIMARY INSURED_____

INS._____POLICY/GROUP#_____PRIMARY INSURED_____

ALLERGIES_____
_____
_____

CURRENT HEALTH ISSUES_____
_____
_____

PAST HEALTH ISSUES _____
_____
_____

CURRENT MEDICATIONS FOR

NAME _____ AGE_____ DOB_____

MEDICATION   **DOSAGE**   **HOW OFTEN**

_____

_____

_____

_____

_____

_____

_____

_____

_____

_____

_____

_____

_____

_____

_____

_____

_____

_____

_____

_____

_____

_____

_____

FAMILY MEDICAL HISTORY

List known medical issues for each section, including
stroke, cancer (type), heart attack, and other major diseases.

WHO (AGE)………………………PROBLEM……...…………………………..

BROTHERS AND SISTERS

_____
_____
_____
_____
_____
_____
_____

PARENTS

_____
_____
_____
_____
_____

MATERNAL GRANDPARENTS

_____
_____
_____
_____
_____

PATERNAL GRANDPARENTS

_____
_____
_____
_____
_____

DATE   TIME   BLOOD PRESSURE PULSE   NOTES   .

DATE	TIME	BLOOD PRESSURE	PULSE	NOTES
_____	_____AM/PM	_____/_____	_____-_____	_____-_____
_____	_____AM/PM	_____/_____	_____-_____	_____-_____
_____	_____AM/PM	_____/_____	_____-_____	_____-_____
_____	_____AM/PM	_____/_____	_____-_____	_____-_____
_____	_____AM/PM	_____/_____	_____-_____	_____-_____
_____	_____AM/PM	_____/_____	_____-_____	_____-_____
_____	_____AM/PM	_____/_____	_____-_____	_____-_____
_____	_____AM/PM	_____/_____	_____-_____	_____-_____
_____	_____AM/PM	_____/_____	_____-_____	_____-_____
_____	_____AM/PM	_____/_____	_____-_____	_____-_____
_____	_____AM/PM	_____/_____	_____-_____	_____-_____
_____	_____AM/PM	_____/_____	_____-_____	_____-_____
_____	_____AM/PM	_____/_____	_____-_____	_____-_____
_____	_____AM/PM	_____/_____	_____-_____	_____-_____
_____	_____AM/PM	_____/_____	_____-_____	_____-_____
_____	_____AM/PM	_____/_____	_____-_____	_____-_____
_____	_____AM/PM	_____/_____	_____-_____	_____-_____
_____	_____AM/PM	_____/_____	_____-_____	_____-_____
_____	_____AM/PM	_____/_____	_____-_____	_____-_____
_____	_____AM/PM	_____/_____	_____-_____	_____-_____
_____	_____AM/PM	_____/_____	_____-_____	_____-_____
_____	_____AM/PM	_____/_____	_____-_____	_____-_____
_____	_____AM/PM	_____/_____	_____-_____	_____-_____
_____	_____AM/PM	_____/_____	_____-_____	_____-_____

Renee' La Viness

Renee' La Viness

DATE	TIME	BLOOD PRESSURE	PULSE	NOTES
_____	_____AM/PM	_____/_____	____-____	____-____ _____
_____	_____AM/PM	_____/_____	____-____	____-____ _____
_____	_____AM/PM	_____/_____	____-____	____-____ _____
_____	_____AM/PM	_____/_____	____-____	____-____ _____
_____	_____AM/PM	_____/_____	____-____	____-____ _____
_____	_____AM/PM	_____/_____	____-____	____-____ _____
_____	_____AM/PM	_____/_____	____-____	____-____ _____
_____	_____AM/PM	_____/_____	____-____	____-____ _____
_____	_____AM/PM	_____/_____	____-____	____-____ _____
_____	_____AM/PM	_____/_____	____-____	____-____ _____
_____	_____AM/PM	_____/_____	____-____	____-____ _____
_____	_____AM/PM	_____/_____	____-____	____-____ _____
_____	_____AM/PM	_____/_____	____-____	____-____ _____
_____	_____AM/PM	_____/_____	____-____	____-____ _____
_____	_____AM/PM	_____/_____	____-____	____-____ _____
_____	_____AM/PM	_____/_____	____-____	____-____ _____
_____	_____AM/PM	_____/_____	____-____	____-____ _____
_____	_____AM/PM	_____/_____	____-____	____-____ _____
_____	_____AM/PM	_____/_____	____-____	____-____ _____
_____	_____AM/PM	_____/_____	____-____	____-____ _____
_____	_____AM/PM	_____/_____	____-____	____-____ _____
_____	_____AM/PM	_____/_____	____-____	____-____ _____
_____	_____AM/PM	_____/_____	____-____	____-____ _____

NAME_____

DATE	TIME	BLOOD PRESSURE	PULSE	NOTES
_____	_____AM/PM	_____ / _____	_____ - _____	_____ - _____
_____	_____AM/PM	_____ / _____	_____ - _____	_____ - _____
_____	_____AM/PM	_____ / _____	_____ - _____	_____ - _____
_____	_____AM/PM	_____ / _____	_____ - _____	_____ - _____
_____	_____AM/PM	_____ / _____	_____ - _____	_____ - _____
_____	_____AM/PM	_____ / _____	_____ - _____	_____ - _____
_____	_____AM/PM	_____ / _____	_____ - _____	_____ - _____
_____	_____AM/PM	_____ / _____	_____ - _____	_____ - _____
_____	_____AM/PM	_____ / _____	_____ - _____	_____ - _____
_____	_____AM/PM	_____ / _____	_____ - _____	_____ - _____
_____	_____AM/PM	_____ / _____	_____ - _____	_____ - _____
_____	_____AM/PM	_____ / _____	_____ - _____	_____ - _____
_____	_____AM/PM	_____ / _____	_____ - _____	_____ - _____
_____	_____AM/PM	_____ / _____	_____ - _____	_____ - _____
_____	_____AM/PM	_____ / _____	_____ - _____	_____ - _____
_____	_____AM/PM	_____ / _____	_____ - _____	_____ - _____
_____	_____AM/PM	_____ / _____	_____ - _____	_____ - _____
_____	_____AM/PM	_____ / _____	_____ - _____	_____ - _____
_____	_____AM/PM	_____ / _____	_____ - _____	_____ - _____
_____	_____AM/PM	_____ / _____	_____ - _____	_____ - _____
_____	_____AM/PM	_____ / _____	_____ - _____	_____ - _____
_____	_____AM/PM	_____ / _____	_____ - _____	_____ - _____
_____	_____AM/PM	_____ / _____	_____ - _____	_____ - _____

DATE	TIME	BLOOD PRESSURE	PULSE	NOTES
_____	_____ AM/PM	_____ / _____	____ - ____	____ - _____
_____	_____ AM/PM	_____ / _____	____ - ____	____ - _____
_____	_____ AM/PM	_____ / _____	____ - ____	____ - _____
_____	_____ AM/PM	_____ / _____	____ - ____	____ - _____
_____	_____ AM/PM	_____ / _____	____ - ____	____ - _____
_____	_____ AM/PM	_____ / _____	____ - ____	____ - _____
_____	_____ AM/PM	_____ / _____	____ - ____	____ - _____
_____	_____ AM/PM	_____ / _____	____ - ____	____ - _____
_____	_____ AM/PM	_____ / _____	____ - ____	____ - _____
_____	_____ AM/PM	_____ / _____	____ - ____	____ - _____
_____	_____ AM/PM	_____ / _____	____ - ____	____ - _____
_____	_____ AM/PM	_____ / _____	____ - ____	____ - _____
_____	_____ AM/PM	_____ / _____	____ - ____	____ - _____
_____	_____ AM/PM	_____ / _____	____ - ____	____ - _____
_____	_____ AM/PM	_____ / _____	____ - ____	____ - _____
_____	_____ AM/PM	_____ / _____	____ - ____	____ - _____
_____	_____ AM/PM	_____ / _____	____ - ____	____ - _____
_____	_____ AM/PM	_____ / _____	____ - ____	____ - _____
_____	_____ AM/PM	_____ / _____	____ - ____	____ - _____
_____	_____ AM/PM	_____ / _____	____ - ____	____ - _____
_____	_____ AM/PM	_____ / _____	____ - ____	____ - _____
_____	_____ AM/PM	_____ / _____	____ - ____	____ - _____
_____	_____ AM/PM	_____ / _____	____ - ____	____ - _____

NAME_____

DATE   TIME   BLOOD PRESSURE PULSE   NOTES

_____ _____AM/PM _____/_____ -_____ -_____ _____

_____ _____AM/PM _____/_____ -_____ -_____ _____

_____ _____AM/PM _____/_____ -_____ -_____ _____

_____ _____AM/PM _____/_____ -_____ -_____ _____

_____ _____AM/PM _____/_____ -_____ -_____ _____

_____ _____AM/PM _____/_____ -_____ -_____ _____

_____ _____AM/PM _____/_____ -_____ -_____ _____

_____ _____AM/PM _____/_____ -_____ -_____ _____

_____ _____AM/PM _____/_____ -_____ -_____ _____

_____ _____AM/PM _____/_____ -_____ -_____ _____

_____ _____AM/PM _____/_____ -_____ -_____ _____

_____ _____AM/PM _____/_____ -_____ -_____ _____

_____ _____AM/PM _____/_____ -_____ -_____ _____

_____ _____AM/PM _____/_____ -_____ -_____ _____

_____ _____AM/PM _____/_____ -_____ -_____ _____

_____ _____AM/PM _____/_____ -_____ -_____ _____

_____ _____AM/PM _____/_____ -_____ -_____ _____

_____ _____AM/PM _____/_____ -_____ -_____ _____

_____ _____AM/PM _____/_____ -_____ -_____ _____

_____ _____AM/PM _____/_____ -_____ -_____ _____

_____ _____AM/PM _____/_____ -_____ -_____ _____

_____ _____AM/PM _____/_____ -_____ -_____ _____

_____ _____AM/PM _____/_____ -_____ -_____ _____

_____ _____AM/PM _____/_____ -_____ -_____ _____

DATE	TIME	BLOOD PRESSURE	PULSE	NOTES
_____	_____AM/PM	_____/_____	___-___	___-___ _____
_____	_____AM/PM	_____/_____	___-___	___-___ _____
_____	_____AM/PM	_____/_____	___-___	___-___ _____
_____	_____AM/PM	_____/_____	___-___	___-___ _____
_____	_____AM/PM	_____/_____	___-___	___-___ _____
_____	_____AM/PM	_____/_____	___-___	___-___ _____
_____	_____AM/PM	_____/_____	___-___	___-___ _____
_____	_____AM/PM	_____/_____	___-___	___-___ _____
_____	_____AM/PM	_____/_____	___-___	___-___ _____
_____	_____AM/PM	_____/_____	___-___	___-___ _____
_____	_____AM/PM	_____/_____	___-___	___-___ _____
_____	_____AM/PM	_____/_____	___-___	___-___ _____
_____	_____AM/PM	_____/_____	___-___	___-___ _____
_____	_____AM/PM	_____/_____	___-___	___-___ _____
_____	_____AM/PM	_____/_____	___-___	___-___ _____
_____	_____AM/PM	_____/_____	___-___	___-___ _____
_____	_____AM/PM	_____/_____	___-___	___-___ _____
_____	_____AM/PM	_____/_____	___-___	___-___ _____
_____	_____AM/PM	_____/_____	___-___	___-___ _____
_____	_____AM/PM	_____/_____	___-___	___-___ _____
_____	_____AM/PM	_____/_____	___-___	___-___ _____
_____	_____AM/PM	_____/_____	___-___	___-___ _____
_____	_____AM/PM	_____/_____	___-___	___-___ _____
_____	_____AM/PM	_____/_____	___-___	___-___ _____

DATE	TIME	BLOOD PRESSURE	PULSE	NOTES
_____	_____AM/PM	_____/_____	____-____	-____ _____
_____	_____AM/PM	_____/_____	____-____	-____ _____
_____	_____AM/PM	_____/_____	____-____	-____ _____
_____	_____AM/PM	_____/_____	____-____	-____ _____
_____	_____AM/PM	_____/_____	____-____	-____ _____
_____	_____AM/PM	_____/_____	____-____	-____ _____
_____	_____AM/PM	_____/_____	____-____	-____ _____
_____	_____AM/PM	_____/_____	____-____	-____ _____
_____	_____AM/PM	_____/_____	____-____	-____ _____
_____	_____AM/PM	_____/_____	____-____	-____ _____
_____	_____AM/PM	_____/_____	____-____	-____ _____
_____	_____AM/PM	_____/_____	____-____	-____ _____
_____	_____AM/PM	_____/_____	____-____	-____ _____
_____	_____AM/PM	_____/_____	____-____	-____ _____
_____	_____AM/PM	_____/_____	____-____	-____ _____
_____	_____AM/PM	_____/_____	____-____	-____ _____
_____	_____AM/PM	_____/_____	____-____	-____ _____
_____	_____AM/PM	_____/_____	____-____	-____ _____
_____	_____AM/PM	_____/_____	____-____	-____ _____
_____	_____AM/PM	_____/_____	____-____	-____ _____
_____	_____AM/PM	_____/_____	____-____	-____ _____
_____	_____AM/PM	_____/_____	____-____	-____ _____
_____	_____AM/PM	_____/_____	____-____	-____ _____
_____	_____AM/PM	_____/_____	____-____	-____ _____

DATE	TIME	BLOOD PRESSURE	PULSE	NOTES
_____	_____AM/PM	_____/_____	____-____ -____	_____
_____	_____AM/PM	_____/_____	____-____ -____	_____
_____	_____AM/PM	_____/_____	____-____ -____	_____
_____	_____AM/PM	_____/_____	____-____ -____	_____
_____	_____AM/PM	_____/_____	____-____ -____	_____
_____	_____AM/PM	_____/_____	____-____ -____	_____
_____	_____AM/PM	_____/_____	____-____ -____	_____
_____	_____AM/PM	_____/_____	____-____ -____	_____
_____	_____AM/PM	_____/_____	____-____ -____	_____
_____	_____AM/PM	_____/_____	____-____ -____	_____
_____	_____AM/PM	_____/_____	____-____ -____	_____
_____	_____AM/PM	_____/_____	____-____ -____	_____
_____	_____AM/PM	_____/_____	____-____ -____	_____
_____	_____AM/PM	_____/_____	____-____ -____	_____
_____	_____AM/PM	_____/_____	____-____ -____	_____
_____	_____AM/PM	_____/_____	____-____ -____	_____
_____	_____AM/PM	_____/_____	____-____ -____	_____
_____	_____AM/PM	_____/_____	____-____ -____	_____
_____	_____AM/PM	_____/_____	____-____ -____	_____
_____	_____AM/PM	_____/_____	____-____ -____	_____
_____	_____AM/PM	_____/_____	____-____ -____	_____
_____	_____AM/PM	_____/_____	____-____ -____	_____
_____	_____AM/PM	_____/_____	____-____ -____	_____
_____	_____AM/PM	_____/_____	____-____ -____	_____

NAME_____

DATE	TIME	BLOOD PRESSURE	PULSE	NOTES
_____	_____ AM/PM	_____ / _____	___ - ___	___ - _____
_____	_____ AM/PM	_____ / _____	___ - ___	___ - _____
_____	_____ AM/PM	_____ / _____	___ - ___	___ - _____
_____	_____ AM/PM	_____ / _____	___ - ___	___ - _____
_____	_____ AM/PM	_____ / _____	___ - ___	___ - _____
_____	_____ AM/PM	_____ / _____	___ - ___	___ - _____
_____	_____ AM/PM	_____ / _____	___ - ___	___ - _____
_____	_____ AM/PM	_____ / _____	___ - ___	___ - _____
_____	_____ AM/PM	_____ / _____	___ - ___	___ - _____
_____	_____ AM/PM	_____ / _____	___ - ___	___ - _____
_____	_____ AM/PM	_____ / _____	___ - ___	___ - _____
_____	_____ AM/PM	_____ / _____	___ - ___	___ - _____
_____	_____ AM/PM	_____ / _____	___ - ___	___ - _____
_____	_____ AM/PM	_____ / _____	___ - ___	___ - _____
_____	_____ AM/PM	_____ / _____	___ - ___	___ - _____
_____	_____ AM/PM	_____ / _____	___ - ___	___ - _____
_____	_____ AM/PM	_____ / _____	___ - ___	___ - _____
_____	_____ AM/PM	_____ / _____	___ - ___	___ - _____
_____	_____ AM/PM	_____ / _____	___ - ___	___ - _____
_____	_____ AM/PM	_____ / _____	___ - ___	___ - _____
_____	_____ AM/PM	_____ / _____	___ - ___	___ - _____
_____	_____ AM/PM	_____ / _____	___ - ___	___ - _____
_____	_____ AM/PM	_____ / _____	___ - ___	___ - _____
_____	_____ AM/PM	_____ / _____	___ - ___	___ - _____
_____	_____ AM/PM	_____ / _____	___ - ___	___ - _____

DATE	TIME	BLOOD PRESSURE	PULSE	NOTES
_____	_____AM/PM	_____/_____	____-____	____-____ _____
_____	_____AM/PM	_____/_____	____-____	____-____ _____
_____	_____AM/PM	_____/_____	____-____	____-____ _____
_____	_____AM/PM	_____/_____	____-____	____-____ _____
_____	_____AM/PM	_____/_____	____-____	____-____ _____
_____	_____AM/PM	_____/_____	____-____	____-____ _____
_____	_____AM/PM	_____/_____	____-____	____-____ _____
_____	_____AM/PM	_____/_____	____-____	____-____ _____
_____	_____AM/PM	_____/_____	____-____	____-____ _____
_____	_____AM/PM	_____/_____	____-____	____-____ _____
_____	_____AM/PM	_____/_____	____-____	____-____ _____
_____	_____AM/PM	_____/_____	____-____	____-____ _____
_____	_____AM/PM	_____/_____	____-____	____-____ _____
_____	_____AM/PM	_____/_____	____-____	____-____ _____
_____	_____AM/PM	_____/_____	____-____	____-____ _____
_____	_____AM/PM	_____/_____	____-____	____-____ _____
_____	_____AM/PM	_____/_____	____-____	____-____ _____
_____	_____AM/PM	_____/_____	____-____	____-____ _____
_____	_____AM/PM	_____/_____	____-____	____-____ _____
_____	_____AM/PM	_____/_____	____-____	____-____ _____
_____	_____AM/PM	_____/_____	____-____	____-____ _____
_____	_____AM/PM	_____/_____	____-____	____-____ _____
_____	_____AM/PM	_____/_____	____-____	____-____ _____
_____	_____AM/PM	_____/_____	____-____	____-____ _____

DATE	TIME	BLOOD PRESSURE	PULSE	NOTES
_____	_____AM/PM	_____/_____	___-___	___-___ _____
_____	_____AM/PM	_____/_____	___-___	___-___ _____
_____	_____AM/PM	_____/_____	___-___	___-___ _____
_____	_____AM/PM	_____/_____	___-___	___-___ _____
_____	_____AM/PM	_____/_____	___-___	___-___ _____
_____	_____AM/PM	_____/_____	___-___	___-___ _____
_____	_____AM/PM	_____/_____	___-___	___-___ _____
_____	_____AM/PM	_____/_____	___-___	___-___ _____
_____	_____AM/PM	_____/_____	___-___	___-___ _____
_____	_____AM/PM	_____/_____	___-___	___-___ _____
_____	_____AM/PM	_____/_____	___-___	___-___ _____
_____	_____AM/PM	_____/_____	___-___	___-___ _____
_____	_____AM/PM	_____/_____	___-___	___-___ _____
_____	_____AM/PM	_____/_____	___-___	___-___ _____
_____	_____AM/PM	_____/_____	___-___	___-___ _____
_____	_____AM/PM	_____/_____	___-___	___-___ _____
_____	_____AM/PM	_____/_____	___-___	___-___ _____
_____	_____AM/PM	_____/_____	___-___	___-___ _____
_____	_____AM/PM	_____/_____	___-___	___-___ _____
_____	_____AM/PM	_____/_____	___-___	___-___ _____
_____	_____AM/PM	_____/_____	___-___	___-___ _____
_____	_____AM/PM	_____/_____	___-___	___-___ _____
_____	_____AM/PM	_____/_____	___-___	___-___ _____
_____	_____AM/PM	_____/_____	___-___	___-___ _____
_____	_____AM/PM	_____/_____	___-___	___-___ _____

DATE	TIME	BLOOD PRESSURE	PULSE	NOTES
_____	_____AM/PM	_____/_____	____-_____	____-_____
_____	_____AM/PM	_____/_____	____-_____	____-_____
_____	_____AM/PM	_____/_____	____-_____	____-_____
_____	_____AM/PM	_____/_____	____-_____	____-_____
_____	_____AM/PM	_____/_____	____-_____	____-_____
_____	_____AM/PM	_____/_____	____-_____	____-_____
_____	_____AM/PM	_____/_____	____-_____	____-_____
_____	_____AM/PM	_____/_____	____-_____	____-_____
_____	_____AM/PM	_____/_____	____-_____	____-_____
_____	_____AM/PM	_____/_____	____-_____	____-_____
_____	_____AM/PM	_____/_____	____-_____	____-_____
_____	_____AM/PM	_____/_____	____-_____	____-_____
_____	_____AM/PM	_____/_____	____-_____	____-_____
_____	_____AM/PM	_____/_____	____-_____	____-_____
_____	_____AM/PM	_____/_____	____-_____	____-_____
_____	_____AM/PM	_____/_____	____-_____	____-_____
_____	_____AM/PM	_____/_____	____-_____	____-_____
_____	_____AM/PM	_____/_____	____-_____	____-_____
_____	_____AM/PM	_____/_____	____-_____	____-_____
_____	_____AM/PM	_____/_____	____-_____	____-_____
_____	_____AM/PM	_____/_____	____-_____	____-_____
_____	_____AM/PM	_____/_____	____-_____	____-_____
_____	_____AM/PM	_____/_____	____-_____	____-_____

DATE   TIME   BLOOD PRESSURE PULSE   NOTES   .

DATE	TIME	BLOOD PRESSURE	PULSE	NOTES
_____	_____ AM/PM	_____ / _____	____ - _____	____ - _____
_____	_____ AM/PM	_____ / _____	____ - _____	____ - _____
_____	_____ AM/PM	_____ / _____	____ - _____	____ - _____
_____	_____ AM/PM	_____ / _____	____ - _____	____ - _____
_____	_____ AM/PM	_____ / _____	____ - _____	____ - _____
_____	_____ AM/PM	_____ / _____	____ - _____	____ - _____
_____	_____ AM/PM	_____ / _____	____ - _____	____ - _____
_____	_____ AM/PM	_____ / _____	____ - _____	____ - _____
_____	_____ AM/PM	_____ / _____	____ - _____	____ - _____
_____	_____ AM/PM	_____ / _____	____ - _____	____ - _____
_____	_____ AM/PM	_____ / _____	____ - _____	____ - _____
_____	_____ AM/PM	_____ / _____	____ - _____	____ - _____
_____	_____ AM/PM	_____ / _____	____ - _____	____ - _____
_____	_____ AM/PM	_____ / _____	____ - _____	____ - _____
_____	_____ AM/PM	_____ / _____	____ - _____	____ - _____
_____	_____ AM/PM	_____ / _____	____ - _____	____ - _____
_____	_____ AM/PM	_____ / _____	____ - _____	____ - _____
_____	_____ AM/PM	_____ / _____	____ - _____	____ - _____
_____	_____ AM/PM	_____ / _____	____ - _____	____ - _____
_____	_____ AM/PM	_____ / _____	____ - _____	____ - _____
_____	_____ AM/PM	_____ / _____	____ - _____	____ - _____
_____	_____ AM/PM	_____ / _____	____ - _____	____ - _____
_____	_____ AM/PM	_____ / _____	____ - _____	____ - _____
_____	_____ AM/PM	_____ / _____	____ - _____	____ - _____

NAME_____

DATE	TIME	BLOOD PRESSURE	PULSE	NOTES
_____	_____AM/PM	_____/_____	___-___	___-___ _____
_____	_____AM/PM	_____/_____	___-___	___-___ _____
_____	_____AM/PM	_____/_____	___-___	___-___ _____
_____	_____AM/PM	_____/_____	___-___	___-___ _____
_____	_____AM/PM	_____/_____	___-___	___-___ _____
_____	_____AM/PM	_____/_____	___-___	___-___ _____
_____	_____AM/PM	_____/_____	___-___	___-___ _____
_____	_____AM/PM	_____/_____	___-___	___-___ _____
_____	_____AM/PM	_____/_____	___-___	___-___ _____
_____	_____AM/PM	_____/_____	___-___	___-___ _____
_____	_____AM/PM	_____/_____	___-___	___-___ _____
_____	_____AM/PM	_____/_____	___-___	___-___ _____
_____	_____AM/PM	_____/_____	___-___	___-___ _____
_____	_____AM/PM	_____/_____	___-___	___-___ _____
_____	_____AM/PM	_____/_____	___-___	___-___ _____
_____	_____AM/PM	_____/_____	___-___	___-___ _____
_____	_____AM/PM	_____/_____	___-___	___-___ _____
_____	_____AM/PM	_____/_____	___-___	___-___ _____
_____	_____AM/PM	_____/_____	___-___	___-___ _____
_____	_____AM/PM	_____/_____	___-___	___-___ _____
_____	_____AM/PM	_____/_____	___-___	___-___ _____
_____	_____AM/PM	_____/_____	___-___	___-___ _____
_____	_____AM/PM	_____/_____	___-___	___-___ _____
_____	_____AM/PM	_____/_____	___-___	___-___ _____

DATE	TIME	BLOOD PRESSURE	PULSE	NOTES
_____	_____AM/PM	_____/_____	___ - ___	_____
_____	_____AM/PM	_____/_____	___ - ___	_____
_____	_____AM/PM	_____/_____	___ - ___	_____
_____	_____AM/PM	_____/_____	___ - ___	_____
_____	_____AM/PM	_____/_____	___ - ___	_____
_____	_____AM/PM	_____/_____	___ - ___	_____
_____	_____AM/PM	_____/_____	___ - ___	_____
_____	_____AM/PM	_____/_____	___ - ___	_____
_____	_____AM/PM	_____/_____	___ - ___	_____
_____	_____AM/PM	_____/_____	___ - ___	_____
_____	_____AM/PM	_____/_____	___ - ___	_____
_____	_____AM/PM	_____/_____	___ - ___	_____
_____	_____AM/PM	_____/_____	___ - ___	_____
_____	_____AM/PM	_____/_____	___ - ___	_____
_____	_____AM/PM	_____/_____	___ - ___	_____
_____	_____AM/PM	_____/_____	___ - ___	_____
_____	_____AM/PM	_____/_____	___ - ___	_____
_____	_____AM/PM	_____/_____	___ - ___	_____
_____	_____AM/PM	_____/_____	___ - ___	_____
_____	_____AM/PM	_____/_____	___ - ___	_____
_____	_____AM/PM	_____/_____	___ - ___	_____
_____	_____AM/PM	_____/_____	___ - ___	_____
_____	_____AM/PM	_____/_____	___ - ___	_____
_____	_____AM/PM	_____/_____	___ - ___	_____

DATE	TIME	BLOOD PRESSURE	PULSE	NOTES
_____	_____AM/PM	_____/_____	_____-_____	_____-_____
_____	_____AM/PM	_____/_____	_____-_____	_____-_____
_____	_____AM/PM	_____/_____	_____-_____	_____-_____
_____	_____AM/PM	_____/_____	_____-_____	_____-_____
_____	_____AM/PM	_____/_____	_____-_____	_____-_____
_____	_____AM/PM	_____/_____	_____-_____	_____-_____
_____	_____AM/PM	_____/_____	_____-_____	_____-_____
_____	_____AM/PM	_____/_____	_____-_____	_____-_____
_____	_____AM/PM	_____/_____	_____-_____	_____-_____
_____	_____AM/PM	_____/_____	_____-_____	_____-_____
_____	_____AM/PM	_____/_____	_____-_____	_____-_____
_____	_____AM/PM	_____/_____	_____-_____	_____-_____
_____	_____AM/PM	_____/_____	_____-_____	_____-_____
_____	_____AM/PM	_____/_____	_____-_____	_____-_____
_____	_____AM/PM	_____/_____	_____-_____	_____-_____
_____	_____AM/PM	_____/_____	_____-_____	_____-_____
_____	_____AM/PM	_____/_____	_____-_____	_____-_____
_____	_____AM/PM	_____/_____	_____-_____	_____-_____
_____	_____AM/PM	_____/_____	_____-_____	_____-_____
_____	_____AM/PM	_____/_____	_____-_____	_____-_____
_____	_____AM/PM	_____/_____	_____-_____	_____-_____
_____	_____AM/PM	_____/_____	_____-_____	_____-_____
_____	_____AM/PM	_____/_____	_____-_____	_____-_____
_____	_____AM/PM	_____/_____	_____-_____	_____-_____

NAME_____

DATE	TIME	BLOOD PRESSURE	PULSE	NOTES
_____	_____ AM/PM	_____ / _____	- _____	- _____
_____	_____ AM/PM	_____ / _____	- _____	- _____
_____	_____ AM/PM	_____ / _____	- _____	- _____
_____	_____ AM/PM	_____ / _____	- _____	- _____
_____	_____ AM/PM	_____ / _____	- _____	- _____
_____	_____ AM/PM	_____ / _____	- _____	- _____
_____	_____ AM/PM	_____ / _____	- _____	- _____
_____	_____ AM/PM	_____ / _____	- _____	- _____
_____	_____ AM/PM	_____ / _____	- _____	- _____
_____	_____ AM/PM	_____ / _____	- _____	- _____
_____	_____ AM/PM	_____ / _____	- _____	- _____
_____	_____ AM/PM	_____ / _____	- _____	- _____
_____	_____ AM/PM	_____ / _____	- _____	- _____
_____	_____ AM/PM	_____ / _____	- _____	- _____
_____	_____ AM/PM	_____ / _____	- _____	- _____
_____	_____ AM/PM	_____ / _____	- _____	- _____
_____	_____ AM/PM	_____ / _____	- _____	- _____
_____	_____ AM/PM	_____ / _____	- _____	- _____
_____	_____ AM/PM	_____ / _____	- _____	- _____
_____	_____ AM/PM	_____ / _____	- _____	- _____
_____	_____ AM/PM	_____ / _____	- _____	- _____
_____	_____ AM/PM	_____ / _____	- _____	- _____
_____	_____ AM/PM	_____ / _____	- _____	- _____
_____	_____ AM/PM	_____ / _____	- _____	- _____

DATE	TIME	BLOOD PRESSURE	PULSE	NOTES
_____	_____ AM/PM	_____ / _____	‐ _____	‐ _____
_____	_____ AM/PM	_____ / _____	‐ _____	‐ _____
_____	_____ AM/PM	_____ / _____	‐ _____	‐ _____
_____	_____ AM/PM	_____ / _____	‐ _____	‐ _____
_____	_____ AM/PM	_____ / _____	‐ _____	‐ _____
_____	_____ AM/PM	_____ / _____	‐ _____	‐ _____
_____	_____ AM/PM	_____ / _____	‐ _____	‐ _____
_____	_____ AM/PM	_____ / _____	‐ _____	‐ _____
_____	_____ AM/PM	_____ / _____	‐ _____	‐ _____
_____	_____ AM/PM	_____ / _____	‐ _____	‐ _____
_____	_____ AM/PM	_____ / _____	‐ _____	‐ _____
_____	_____ AM/PM	_____ / _____	‐ _____	‐ _____
_____	_____ AM/PM	_____ / _____	‐ _____	‐ _____
_____	_____ AM/PM	_____ / _____	‐ _____	‐ _____
_____	_____ AM/PM	_____ / _____	‐ _____	‐ _____
_____	_____ AM/PM	_____ / _____	‐ _____	‐ _____
_____	_____ AM/PM	_____ / _____	‐ _____	‐ _____
_____	_____ AM/PM	_____ / _____	‐ _____	‐ _____
_____	_____ AM/PM	_____ / _____	‐ _____	‐ _____
_____	_____ AM/PM	_____ / _____	‐ _____	‐ _____
_____	_____ AM/PM	_____ / _____	‐ _____	‐ _____
_____	_____ AM/PM	_____ / _____	‐ _____	‐ _____
_____	_____ AM/PM	_____ / _____	‐ _____	‐ _____
_____	_____ AM/PM	_____ / _____	‐ _____	‐ _____

DATE	TIME	BLOOD PRESSURE	PULSE	NOTES
_____	_____ AM/PM	_____ / _____	_____ - _____	_____ - _____
_____	_____ AM/PM	_____ / _____	_____ - _____	_____ - _____
_____	_____ AM/PM	_____ / _____	_____ - _____	_____ - _____
_____	_____ AM/PM	_____ / _____	_____ - _____	_____ - _____
_____	_____ AM/PM	_____ / _____	_____ - _____	_____ - _____
_____	_____ AM/PM	_____ / _____	_____ - _____	_____ - _____
_____	_____ AM/PM	_____ / _____	_____ - _____	_____ - _____
_____	_____ AM/PM	_____ / _____	_____ - _____	_____ - _____
_____	_____ AM/PM	_____ / _____	_____ - _____	_____ - _____
_____	_____ AM/PM	_____ / _____	_____ - _____	_____ - _____
_____	_____ AM/PM	_____ / _____	_____ - _____	_____ - _____
_____	_____ AM/PM	_____ / _____	_____ - _____	_____ - _____
_____	_____ AM/PM	_____ / _____	_____ - _____	_____ - _____
_____	_____ AM/PM	_____ / _____	_____ - _____	_____ - _____
_____	_____ AM/PM	_____ / _____	_____ - _____	_____ - _____
_____	_____ AM/PM	_____ / _____	_____ - _____	_____ - _____
_____	_____ AM/PM	_____ / _____	_____ - _____	_____ - _____
_____	_____ AM/PM	_____ / _____	_____ - _____	_____ - _____
_____	_____ AM/PM	_____ / _____	_____ - _____	_____ - _____
_____	_____ AM/PM	_____ / _____	_____ - _____	_____ - _____
_____	_____ AM/PM	_____ / _____	_____ - _____	_____ - _____
_____	_____ AM/PM	_____ / _____	_____ - _____	_____ - _____
_____	_____ AM/PM	_____ / _____	_____ - _____	_____ - _____

DATE	TIME	BLOOD PRESSURE	PULSE	NOTES
_____	_____AM/PM	_____ / _____	- _____	- _____
_____	_____AM/PM	_____ / _____	- _____	- _____
_____	_____AM/PM	_____ / _____	- _____	- _____
_____	_____AM/PM	_____ / _____	- _____	- _____
_____	_____AM/PM	_____ / _____	- _____	- _____
_____	_____AM/PM	_____ / _____	- _____	- _____
_____	_____AM/PM	_____ / _____	- _____	- _____
_____	_____AM/PM	_____ / _____	- _____	- _____
_____	_____AM/PM	_____ / _____	- _____	- _____
_____	_____AM/PM	_____ / _____	- _____	- _____
_____	_____AM/PM	_____ / _____	- _____	- _____
_____	_____AM/PM	_____ / _____	- _____	- _____
_____	_____AM/PM	_____ / _____	- _____	- _____
_____	_____AM/PM	_____ / _____	- _____	- _____
_____	_____AM/PM	_____ / _____	- _____	- _____
_____	_____AM/PM	_____ / _____	- _____	- _____
_____	_____AM/PM	_____ / _____	- _____	- _____
_____	_____AM/PM	_____ / _____	- _____	- _____
_____	_____AM/PM	_____ / _____	- _____	- _____
_____	_____AM/PM	_____ / _____	- _____	- _____
_____	_____AM/PM	_____ / _____	- _____	- _____
_____	_____AM/PM	_____ / _____	- _____	- _____
_____	_____AM/PM	_____ / _____	- _____	- _____

DATE	TIME	BLOOD PRESSURE	PULSE	NOTES
_____	_____AM/PM	_____ / _____	____ - ____	____ - _____
_____	_____AM/PM	_____ / _____	____ - ____	____ - _____
_____	_____AM/PM	_____ / _____	____ - ____	____ - _____
_____	_____AM/PM	_____ / _____	____ - ____	____ - _____
_____	_____AM/PM	_____ / _____	____ - ____	____ - _____
_____	_____AM/PM	_____ / _____	____ - ____	____ - _____
_____	_____AM/PM	_____ / _____	____ - ____	____ - _____
_____	_____AM/PM	_____ / _____	____ - ____	____ - _____
_____	_____AM/PM	_____ / _____	____ - ____	____ - _____
_____	_____AM/PM	_____ / _____	____ - ____	____ - _____
_____	_____AM/PM	_____ / _____	____ - ____	____ - _____
_____	_____AM/PM	_____ / _____	____ - ____	____ - _____
_____	_____AM/PM	_____ / _____	____ - ____	____ - _____
_____	_____AM/PM	_____ / _____	____ - ____	____ - _____
_____	_____AM/PM	_____ / _____	____ - ____	____ - _____
_____	_____AM/PM	_____ / _____	____ - ____	____ - _____
_____	_____AM/PM	_____ / _____	____ - ____	____ - _____
_____	_____AM/PM	_____ / _____	____ - ____	____ - _____
_____	_____AM/PM	_____ / _____	____ - ____	____ - _____
_____	_____AM/PM	_____ / _____	____ - ____	____ - _____
_____	_____AM/PM	_____ / _____	____ - ____	____ - _____
_____	_____AM/PM	_____ / _____	____ - ____	____ - _____
_____	_____AM/PM	_____ / _____	____ - ____	____ - _____
_____	_____AM/PM	_____ / _____	____ - ____	____ - _____

Renee' La Viness

Renee' La Viness

DATE	TIME	BLOOD PRESSURE	PULSE	NOTES
_____	_____AM/PM	_____/_____	___ - _____	___ - _____
_____	_____AM/PM	_____/_____	___ - _____	___ - _____
_____	_____AM/PM	_____/_____	___ - _____	___ - _____
_____	_____AM/PM	_____/_____	___ - _____	___ - _____
_____	_____AM/PM	_____/_____	___ - _____	___ - _____
_____	_____AM/PM	_____/_____	___ - _____	___ - _____
_____	_____AM/PM	_____/_____	___ - _____	___ - _____
_____	_____AM/PM	_____/_____	___ - _____	___ - _____
_____	_____AM/PM	_____/_____	___ - _____	___ - _____
_____	_____AM/PM	_____/_____	___ - _____	___ - _____
_____	_____AM/PM	_____/_____	___ - _____	___ - _____
_____	_____AM/PM	_____/_____	___ - _____	___ - _____
_____	_____AM/PM	_____/_____	___ - _____	___ - _____
_____	_____AM/PM	_____/_____	___ - _____	___ - _____
_____	_____AM/PM	_____/_____	___ - _____	___ - _____
_____	_____AM/PM	_____/_____	___ - _____	___ - _____
_____	_____AM/PM	_____/_____	___ - _____	___ - _____
_____	_____AM/PM	_____/_____	___ - _____	___ - _____
_____	_____AM/PM	_____/_____	___ - _____	___ - _____
_____	_____AM/PM	_____/_____	___ - _____	___ - _____
_____	_____AM/PM	_____/_____	___ - _____	___ - _____
_____	_____AM/PM	_____/_____	___ - _____	___ - _____
_____	_____AM/PM	_____/_____	___ - _____	___ - _____
_____	_____AM/PM	_____/_____	___ - _____	___ - _____

DATE	TIME	BLOOD PRESSURE	PULSE	NOTES
_____	_____ AM/PM	_____ / _____	- _____	- _____
_____	_____ AM/PM	_____ / _____	- _____	- _____
_____	_____ AM/PM	_____ / _____	- _____	- _____
_____	_____ AM/PM	_____ / _____	- _____	- _____
_____	_____ AM/PM	_____ / _____	- _____	- _____
_____	_____ AM/PM	_____ / _____	- _____	- _____
_____	_____ AM/PM	_____ / _____	- _____	- _____
_____	_____ AM/PM	_____ / _____	- _____	- _____
_____	_____ AM/PM	_____ / _____	- _____	- _____
_____	_____ AM/PM	_____ / _____	- _____	- _____
_____	_____ AM/PM	_____ / _____	- _____	- _____
_____	_____ AM/PM	_____ / _____	- _____	- _____
_____	_____ AM/PM	_____ / _____	- _____	- _____
_____	_____ AM/PM	_____ / _____	- _____	- _____
_____	_____ AM/PM	_____ / _____	- _____	- _____
_____	_____ AM/PM	_____ / _____	- _____	- _____
_____	_____ AM/PM	_____ / _____	- _____	- _____
_____	_____ AM/PM	_____ / _____	- _____	- _____
_____	_____ AM/PM	_____ / _____	- _____	- _____
_____	_____ AM/PM	_____ / _____	- _____	- _____
_____	_____ AM/PM	_____ / _____	- _____	- _____
_____	_____ AM/PM	_____ / _____	- _____	- _____
_____	_____ AM/PM	_____ / _____	- _____	- _____
_____	_____ AM/PM	_____ / _____	- _____	- _____

DATE   TIME   BLOOD PRESSURE PULSE   NOTES   .

DATE	TIME	BLOOD PRESSURE	PULSE	NOTES
_____	_____ AM/PM	_____ / _____	- _____	- _____
_____	_____ AM/PM	_____ / _____	- _____	- _____
_____	_____ AM/PM	_____ / _____	- _____	- _____
_____	_____ AM/PM	_____ / _____	- _____	- _____
_____	_____ AM/PM	_____ / _____	- _____	- _____
_____	_____ AM/PM	_____ / _____	- _____	- _____
_____	_____ AM/PM	_____ / _____	- _____	- _____
_____	_____ AM/PM	_____ / _____	- _____	- _____
_____	_____ AM/PM	_____ / _____	- _____	- _____
_____	_____ AM/PM	_____ / _____	- _____	- _____
_____	_____ AM/PM	_____ / _____	- _____	- _____
_____	_____ AM/PM	_____ / _____	- _____	- _____
_____	_____ AM/PM	_____ / _____	- _____	- _____
_____	_____ AM/PM	_____ / _____	- _____	- _____
_____	_____ AM/PM	_____ / _____	- _____	- _____
_____	_____ AM/PM	_____ / _____	- _____	- _____
_____	_____ AM/PM	_____ / _____	- _____	- _____
_____	_____ AM/PM	_____ / _____	- _____	- _____
_____	_____ AM/PM	_____ / _____	- _____	- _____
_____	_____ AM/PM	_____ / _____	- _____	- _____
_____	_____ AM/PM	_____ / _____	- _____	- _____
_____	_____ AM/PM	_____ / _____	- _____	- _____
_____	_____ AM/PM	_____ / _____	- _____	- _____

DATE	TIME	BLOOD PRESSURE	PULSE	NOTES
_____	_____AM/PM	_____/_____	___-___	___-___ _____
_____	_____AM/PM	_____/_____	___-___	___-___ _____
_____	_____AM/PM	_____/_____	___-___	___-___ _____
_____	_____AM/PM	_____/_____	___-___	___-___ _____
_____	_____AM/PM	_____/_____	___-___	___-___ _____
_____	_____AM/PM	_____/_____	___-___	___-___ _____
_____	_____AM/PM	_____/_____	___-___	___-___ _____
_____	_____AM/PM	_____/_____	___-___	___-___ _____
_____	_____AM/PM	_____/_____	___-___	___-___ _____
_____	_____AM/PM	_____/_____	___-___	___-___ _____
_____	_____AM/PM	_____/_____	___-___	___-___ _____
_____	_____AM/PM	_____/_____	___-___	___-___ _____
_____	_____AM/PM	_____/_____	___-___	___-___ _____
_____	_____AM/PM	_____/_____	___-___	___-___ _____
_____	_____AM/PM	_____/_____	___-___	___-___ _____
_____	_____AM/PM	_____/_____	___-___	___-___ _____
_____	_____AM/PM	_____/_____	___-___	___-___ _____
_____	_____AM/PM	_____/_____	___-___	___-___ _____
_____	_____AM/PM	_____/_____	___-___	___-___ _____
_____	_____AM/PM	_____/_____	___-___	___-___ _____
_____	_____AM/PM	_____/_____	___-___	___-___ _____
_____	_____AM/PM	_____/_____	___-___	___-___ _____
_____	_____AM/PM	_____/_____	___-___	___-___ _____
_____	_____AM/PM	_____/_____	___-___	___-___ _____

DATE	TIME	BLOOD PRESSURE	PULSE	NOTES
_____	_____ AM/PM	_____ / _____	_____ - _____	_____ - _____
_____	_____ AM/PM	_____ / _____	_____ - _____	_____ - _____
_____	_____ AM/PM	_____ / _____	_____ - _____	_____ - _____
_____	_____ AM/PM	_____ / _____	_____ - _____	_____ - _____
_____	_____ AM/PM	_____ / _____	_____ - _____	_____ - _____
_____	_____ AM/PM	_____ / _____	_____ - _____	_____ - _____
_____	_____ AM/PM	_____ / _____	_____ - _____	_____ - _____
_____	_____ AM/PM	_____ / _____	_____ - _____	_____ - _____
_____	_____ AM/PM	_____ / _____	_____ - _____	_____ - _____
_____	_____ AM/PM	_____ / _____	_____ - _____	_____ - _____
_____	_____ AM/PM	_____ / _____	_____ - _____	_____ - _____
_____	_____ AM/PM	_____ / _____	_____ - _____	_____ - _____
_____	_____ AM/PM	_____ / _____	_____ - _____	_____ - _____
_____	_____ AM/PM	_____ / _____	_____ - _____	_____ - _____
_____	_____ AM/PM	_____ / _____	_____ - _____	_____ - _____
_____	_____ AM/PM	_____ / _____	_____ - _____	_____ - _____
_____	_____ AM/PM	_____ / _____	_____ - _____	_____ - _____
_____	_____ AM/PM	_____ / _____	_____ - _____	_____ - _____
_____	_____ AM/PM	_____ / _____	_____ - _____	_____ - _____
_____	_____ AM/PM	_____ / _____	_____ - _____	_____ - _____
_____	_____ AM/PM	_____ / _____	_____ - _____	_____ - _____
_____	_____ AM/PM	_____ / _____	_____ - _____	_____ - _____
_____	_____ AM/PM	_____ / _____	_____ - _____	_____ - _____
_____	_____ AM/PM	_____ / _____	_____ - _____	_____ - _____

DATE	TIME	BLOOD PRESSURE	PULSE	NOTES
_____	_____AM/PM	_____/_____	____ - _____	____ - _____
_____	_____AM/PM	_____/_____	____ - _____	____ - _____
_____	_____AM/PM	_____/_____	____ - _____	____ - _____
_____	_____AM/PM	_____/_____	____ - _____	____ - _____
_____	_____AM/PM	_____/_____	____ - _____	____ - _____
_____	_____AM/PM	_____/_____	____ - _____	____ - _____
_____	_____AM/PM	_____/_____	____ - _____	____ - _____
_____	_____AM/PM	_____/_____	____ - _____	____ - _____
_____	_____AM/PM	_____/_____	____ - _____	____ - _____
_____	_____AM/PM	_____/_____	____ - _____	____ - _____
_____	_____AM/PM	_____/_____	____ - _____	____ - _____
_____	_____AM/PM	_____/_____	____ - _____	____ - _____
_____	_____AM/PM	_____/_____	____ - _____	____ - _____
_____	_____AM/PM	_____/_____	____ - _____	____ - _____
_____	_____AM/PM	_____/_____	____ - _____	____ - _____
_____	_____AM/PM	_____/_____	____ - _____	____ - _____
_____	_____AM/PM	_____/_____	____ - _____	____ - _____
_____	_____AM/PM	_____/_____	____ - _____	____ - _____
_____	_____AM/PM	_____/_____	____ - _____	____ - _____
_____	_____AM/PM	_____/_____	____ - _____	____ - _____
_____	_____AM/PM	_____/_____	____ - _____	____ - _____
_____	_____AM/PM	_____/_____	____ - _____	____ - _____
_____	_____AM/PM	_____/_____	____ - _____	____ - _____
_____	_____AM/PM	_____/_____	____ - _____	____ - _____

NAME_____

DATE	TIME	BLOOD PRESSURE	PULSE	NOTES
_____	_____ AM/PM	_____ / _____	____ - ____	____ - _____
_____	_____ AM/PM	_____ / _____	____ - ____	____ - _____
_____	_____ AM/PM	_____ / _____	____ - ____	____ - _____
_____	_____ AM/PM	_____ / _____	____ - ____	____ - _____
_____	_____ AM/PM	_____ / _____	____ - ____	____ - _____
_____	_____ AM/PM	_____ / _____	____ - ____	____ - _____
_____	_____ AM/PM	_____ / _____	____ - ____	____ - _____
_____	_____ AM/PM	_____ / _____	____ - ____	____ - _____
_____	_____ AM/PM	_____ / _____	____ - ____	____ - _____
_____	_____ AM/PM	_____ / _____	____ - ____	____ - _____
_____	_____ AM/PM	_____ / _____	____ - ____	____ - _____
_____	_____ AM/PM	_____ / _____	____ - ____	____ - _____
_____	_____ AM/PM	_____ / _____	____ - ____	____ - _____
_____	_____ AM/PM	_____ / _____	____ - ____	____ - _____
_____	_____ AM/PM	_____ / _____	____ - ____	____ - _____
_____	_____ AM/PM	_____ / _____	____ - ____	____ - _____
_____	_____ AM/PM	_____ / _____	____ - ____	____ - _____
_____	_____ AM/PM	_____ / _____	____ - ____	____ - _____
_____	_____ AM/PM	_____ / _____	____ - ____	____ - _____
_____	_____ AM/PM	_____ / _____	____ - ____	____ - _____
_____	_____ AM/PM	_____ / _____	____ - ____	____ - _____
_____	_____ AM/PM	_____ / _____	____ - ____	____ - _____
_____	_____ AM/PM	_____ / _____	____ - ____	____ - _____
_____	_____ AM/PM	_____ / _____	____ - ____	____ - _____

DATE	TIME	BLOOD PRESSURE	PULSE	NOTES
_____	_____AM/PM	_____/_____	___-_____	___-_____
_____	_____AM/PM	_____/_____	___-_____	___-_____
_____	_____AM/PM	_____/_____	___-_____	___-_____
_____	_____AM/PM	_____/_____	___-_____	___-_____
_____	_____AM/PM	_____/_____	___-_____	___-_____
_____	_____AM/PM	_____/_____	___-_____	___-_____
_____	_____AM/PM	_____/_____	___-_____	___-_____
_____	_____AM/PM	_____/_____	___-_____	___-_____
_____	_____AM/PM	_____/_____	___-_____	___-_____
_____	_____AM/PM	_____/_____	___-_____	___-_____
_____	_____AM/PM	_____/_____	___-_____	___-_____
_____	_____AM/PM	_____/_____	___-_____	___-_____
_____	_____AM/PM	_____/_____	___-_____	___-_____
_____	_____AM/PM	_____/_____	___-_____	___-_____
_____	_____AM/PM	_____/_____	___-_____	___-_____
_____	_____AM/PM	_____/_____	___-_____	___-_____
_____	_____AM/PM	_____/_____	___-_____	___-_____
_____	_____AM/PM	_____/_____	___-_____	___-_____
_____	_____AM/PM	_____/_____	___-_____	___-_____
_____	_____AM/PM	_____/_____	___-_____	___-_____
_____	_____AM/PM	_____/_____	___-_____	___-_____
_____	_____AM/PM	_____/_____	___-_____	___-_____
_____	_____AM/PM	_____/_____	___-_____	___-_____

DATE	TIME	BLOOD PRESSURE	PULSE	NOTES
_____	_____AM/PM	_____/_____	- _____	- _____
_____	_____AM/PM	_____/_____	- _____	- _____
_____	_____AM/PM	_____/_____	- _____	- _____
_____	_____AM/PM	_____/_____	- _____	- _____
_____	_____AM/PM	_____/_____	- _____	- _____
_____	_____AM/PM	_____/_____	- _____	- _____
_____	_____AM/PM	_____/_____	- _____	- _____
_____	_____AM/PM	_____/_____	- _____	- _____
_____	_____AM/PM	_____/_____	- _____	- _____
_____	_____AM/PM	_____/_____	- _____	- _____
_____	_____AM/PM	_____/_____	- _____	- _____
_____	_____AM/PM	_____/_____	- _____	- _____
_____	_____AM/PM	_____/_____	- _____	- _____
_____	_____AM/PM	_____/_____	- _____	- _____
_____	_____AM/PM	_____/_____	- _____	- _____
_____	_____AM/PM	_____/_____	- _____	- _____
_____	_____AM/PM	_____/_____	- _____	- _____
_____	_____AM/PM	_____/_____	- _____	- _____
_____	_____AM/PM	_____/_____	- _____	- _____
_____	_____AM/PM	_____/_____	- _____	- _____
_____	_____AM/PM	_____/_____	- _____	- _____
_____	_____AM/PM	_____/_____	- _____	- _____
_____	_____AM/PM	_____/_____	- _____	- _____
_____	_____AM/PM	_____/_____	- _____	- _____

DATE	TIME	BLOOD PRESSURE	PULSE	NOTES
_____	_____AM/PM	_____/_____	____-____	____-____
_____	_____AM/PM	_____/_____	____-____	____-____
_____	_____AM/PM	_____/_____	____-____	____-____
_____	_____AM/PM	_____/_____	____-____	____-____
_____	_____AM/PM	_____/_____	____-____	____-____
_____	_____AM/PM	_____/_____	____-____	____-____
_____	_____AM/PM	_____/_____	____-____	____-____
_____	_____AM/PM	_____/_____	____-____	____-____
_____	_____AM/PM	_____/_____	____-____	____-____
_____	_____AM/PM	_____/_____	____-____	____-____
_____	_____AM/PM	_____/_____	____-____	____-____
_____	_____AM/PM	_____/_____	____-____	____-____
_____	_____AM/PM	_____/_____	____-____	____-____
_____	_____AM/PM	_____/_____	____-____	____-____
_____	_____AM/PM	_____/_____	____-____	____-____
_____	_____AM/PM	_____/_____	____-____	____-____
_____	_____AM/PM	_____/_____	____-____	____-____
_____	_____AM/PM	_____/_____	____-____	____-____
_____	_____AM/PM	_____/_____	____-____	____-____
_____	_____AM/PM	_____/_____	____-____	____-____
_____	_____AM/PM	_____/_____	____-____	____-____
_____	_____AM/PM	_____/_____	____-____	____-____
_____	_____AM/PM	_____/_____	____-____	____-____
_____	_____AM/PM	_____/_____	____-____	____-____

DATE	TIME	BLOOD PRESSURE	PULSE	NOTES
_____	_____AM/PM	_____/_____	_____-_____	_____-_____ _____
_____	_____AM/PM	_____/_____	_____-_____	_____-_____ _____
_____	_____AM/PM	_____/_____	_____-_____	_____-_____ _____
_____	_____AM/PM	_____/_____	_____-_____	_____-_____ _____
_____	_____AM/PM	_____/_____	_____-_____	_____-_____ _____
_____	_____AM/PM	_____/_____	_____-_____	_____-_____ _____
_____	_____AM/PM	_____/_____	_____-_____	_____-_____ _____
_____	_____AM/PM	_____/_____	_____-_____	_____-_____ _____
_____	_____AM/PM	_____/_____	_____-_____	_____-_____ _____
_____	_____AM/PM	_____/_____	_____-_____	_____-_____ _____
_____	_____AM/PM	_____/_____	_____-_____	_____-_____ _____
_____	_____AM/PM	_____/_____	_____-_____	_____-_____ _____
_____	_____AM/PM	_____/_____	_____-_____	_____-_____ _____
_____	_____AM/PM	_____/_____	_____-_____	_____-_____ _____
_____	_____AM/PM	_____/_____	_____-_____	_____-_____ _____
_____	_____AM/PM	_____/_____	_____-_____	_____-_____ _____
_____	_____AM/PM	_____/_____	_____-_____	_____-_____ _____
_____	_____AM/PM	_____/_____	_____-_____	_____-_____ _____
_____	_____AM/PM	_____/_____	_____-_____	_____-_____ _____
_____	_____AM/PM	_____/_____	_____-_____	_____-_____ _____
_____	_____AM/PM	_____/_____	_____-_____	_____-_____ _____
_____	_____AM/PM	_____/_____	_____-_____	_____-_____ _____
_____	_____AM/PM	_____/_____	_____-_____	_____-_____ _____
_____	_____AM/PM	_____/_____	_____-_____	_____-_____ _____

DATE	TIME	BLOOD PRESSURE	PULSE	NOTES
_____	_____AM/PM	_____/_____	_____-_____	_____
_____	_____AM/PM	_____/_____	_____-_____	_____
_____	_____AM/PM	_____/_____	_____-_____	_____
_____	_____AM/PM	_____/_____	_____-_____	_____
_____	_____AM/PM	_____/_____	_____-_____	_____
_____	_____AM/PM	_____/_____	_____-_____	_____
_____	_____AM/PM	_____/_____	_____-_____	_____
_____	_____AM/PM	_____/_____	_____-_____	_____
_____	_____AM/PM	_____/_____	_____-_____	_____
_____	_____AM/PM	_____/_____	_____-_____	_____
_____	_____AM/PM	_____/_____	_____-_____	_____
_____	_____AM/PM	_____/_____	_____-_____	_____
_____	_____AM/PM	_____/_____	_____-_____	_____
_____	_____AM/PM	_____/_____	_____-_____	_____
_____	_____AM/PM	_____/_____	_____-_____	_____
_____	_____AM/PM	_____/_____	_____-_____	_____
_____	_____AM/PM	_____/_____	_____-_____	_____
_____	_____AM/PM	_____/_____	_____-_____	_____
_____	_____AM/PM	_____/_____	_____-_____	_____
_____	_____AM/PM	_____/_____	_____-_____	_____
_____	_____AM/PM	_____/_____	_____-_____	_____
_____	_____AM/PM	_____/_____	_____-_____	_____
_____	_____AM/PM	_____/_____	_____-_____	_____
_____	_____AM/PM	_____/_____	_____-_____	_____

NAME_____

DATE	TIME	BLOOD PRESSURE	PULSE	NOTES
_____	_____AM/PM	_____ / _____	___ - ___	___ - _____
_____	_____AM/PM	_____ / _____	___ - ___	___ - _____
_____	_____AM/PM	_____ / _____	___ - ___	___ - _____
_____	_____AM/PM	_____ / _____	___ - ___	___ - _____
_____	_____AM/PM	_____ / _____	___ - ___	___ - _____
_____	_____AM/PM	_____ / _____	___ - ___	___ - _____
_____	_____AM/PM	_____ / _____	___ - ___	___ - _____
_____	_____AM/PM	_____ / _____	___ - ___	___ - _____
_____	_____AM/PM	_____ / _____	___ - ___	___ - _____
_____	_____AM/PM	_____ / _____	___ - ___	___ - _____
_____	_____AM/PM	_____ / _____	___ - ___	___ - _____
_____	_____AM/PM	_____ / _____	___ - ___	___ - _____
_____	_____AM/PM	_____ / _____	___ - ___	___ - _____
_____	_____AM/PM	_____ / _____	___ - ___	___ - _____
_____	_____AM/PM	_____ / _____	___ - ___	___ - _____
_____	_____AM/PM	_____ / _____	___ - ___	___ - _____
_____	_____AM/PM	_____ / _____	___ - ___	___ - _____
_____	_____AM/PM	_____ / _____	___ - ___	___ - _____
_____	_____AM/PM	_____ / _____	___ - ___	___ - _____
_____	_____AM/PM	_____ / _____	___ - ___	___ - _____
_____	_____AM/PM	_____ / _____	___ - ___	___ - _____
_____	_____AM/PM	_____ / _____	___ - ___	___ - _____
_____	_____AM/PM	_____ / _____	___ - ___	___ - _____
_____	_____AM/PM	_____ / _____	___ - ___	___ - _____

DATE	TIME	BLOOD PRESSURE	PULSE	NOTES
_____	_____AM/PM	_____/_____	_____-_____	-_____
_____	_____AM/PM	_____/_____	_____-_____	-_____
_____	_____AM/PM	_____/_____	_____-_____	-_____
_____	_____AM/PM	_____/_____	_____-_____	-_____
_____	_____AM/PM	_____/_____	_____-_____	-_____
_____	_____AM/PM	_____/_____	_____-_____	-_____
_____	_____AM/PM	_____/_____	_____-_____	-_____
_____	_____AM/PM	_____/_____	_____-_____	-_____
_____	_____AM/PM	_____/_____	_____-_____	-_____
_____	_____AM/PM	_____/_____	_____-_____	-_____
_____	_____AM/PM	_____/_____	_____-_____	-_____
_____	_____AM/PM	_____/_____	_____-_____	-_____
_____	_____AM/PM	_____/_____	_____-_____	-_____
_____	_____AM/PM	_____/_____	_____-_____	-_____
_____	_____AM/PM	_____/_____	_____-_____	-_____
_____	_____AM/PM	_____/_____	_____-_____	-_____
_____	_____AM/PM	_____/_____	_____-_____	-_____
_____	_____AM/PM	_____/_____	_____-_____	-_____
_____	_____AM/PM	_____/_____	_____-_____	-_____
_____	_____AM/PM	_____/_____	_____-_____	-_____
_____	_____AM/PM	_____/_____	_____-_____	-_____
_____	_____AM/PM	_____/_____	_____-_____	-_____
_____	_____AM/PM	_____/_____	_____-_____	-_____